OUR SCHOOLS AND COLLEGES.

BY REV. JOHN T. HUNTINGTON,

PROFESSOR OF GREEK AT TRINITY COLLEGE, HARTFORD, CONNECTICUT.

REPUBLISHED BY REQUEST OF SEVERAL BISHOPS AND PRESBYTERS AND LAYMEN, FROM THE JULY NO. OF THE "CHURCH MONTHLY."

BOSTON:

McINTIRE & MOULTON, PRINTERS, 42 CONGRESS STREET.

1866.

OUR

SCHOOLS

AND

COLLEGES.

BY REV. JOHN T. HUNTINGTON,

PROFESSOR OF GREEK AT TRINITY COLLEGE, HARTFORD, CONNECTICUT.

REPUBLISHED BY REQUEST OF SEVERAL BISHOPS AND PRESBYTERS AND LAYMEN, FROM THE JULY NO. OF THE "CHURCH MONTHLY."

BOSTON:

McINTIRE & MOULTON, PRINTERS, 42 CONGRESS STREET.

1866.

OUR SCHOOLS AND COLLEGES.*

A QUARTER of a century ago a distinguished writer on education exclaimed, "Educational science is yet in all the rubbish and disorder of discovery." Locke, in his generation, had exposed some of its humbugs in England; Rousseau did his part in France: but before Pestalozzi's day, and long after, education in Europe was a sort of quackery. The monitorial systems of Bell and Lancaster had to be carried out in baskets full and buried; the Gradgrinds and Ichabod Cranes ceased to be our ideal school masters; "the three R.'s" failed to complete the school curriculum; and an ability to translate in the class-room a well-conned passage from Cicero or Homer ceased to be the acme of the college course. But, although much has been accomplished, a great deal remains to be done. The rubbish has been only partially removed; and we have but just reached the foundations on which education, as a science, rests.

* Catalogue of Trinity College, 1865–6; of Hobart College, 1865–6; of Kenyon College, 1865–6; of Racine College, 1865–6; of Griswold College, 1865–6; of Columbia College, 1865–6; of Norwich University, Vt.; of St. Paul's School, Concord, N. H.; of Cheshire Academy, Conn.; of Rectory School, Hamden, Conn.; of Deer-Hill Institute, Danbury, Conn.; of St. Paul's School, Brookfield, Conn.; of the Berkley School, Middletown, Conn.; of the Divinity School, Philadelphia; of the General Theological Seminary, New York.

Such questions as the following are now asked by parents and guardians: "What is a true education?"— "Is it intellectual culture alone?" — "Can a Unitarian or a Universalist or a Jesuit educate our sons and daughters?" — "Do the Catechism, and a few chapters recited in Bible-class, and the eloquent or profound or prosy sermons weekly, — do these constitute all the religious education which our coming statesmen and bishops and presbyters require?" — "Is facility at a stump-speech education?" — "Is the present low condition of genuine piety and self-devotion, and information on Church subjects in all our parishes, — is this education?" We are disposed to answer all these queries with an emphatic "No;" while, at the same time, we feel very thankful for such an exhibition of inquisitiveness in regard to so important a subject as Christian education.

The growing list of schools and colleges — which heads our article — is farther proof that the mind of the Church is waking up to the demands of the country upon us as a branch of the Church Catholic; and the enthusiastic reception, by the late General Convention, of the Report of the Standing Committee on Christian Education, is added witness to the wide-spread interest that to-day exists in the American Church. Every teacher should carefully read this most suggestive Report, and then endeavor to answer, more fully than we now have space for, some of the questions above asked. And, first, "What is true, healthy education for American boys and girls?" Peculiar advantages, and special responsibilities attached to them, are given to the youth of our wide country, — the home of free thought and free speech. Hence we would argue, if it were not too obvious for argument, that a Continental or a German culture exclusively, or a French finish, or even a pure English education, is not the exact model for Americans. We do not want Germanized colleges nor Frenchified schools, for which the rage is at present. We want no such profundity as the most finished scholars and deepest thinkers of Tübingen and Heidelberg flounder in, endlessly debating the supreme importance of the difference between "the I and the not I." But we do want the rare intellectuality and the fearlessness in search of truth, united with the mighty lesson which German scholars have taught the world during the last decade, viz., that "the wisdom of this world is foolishness with God." We want also the grace and refinement that inheres, spite of all the taints of false philosophy, in the literature of *la belle France:* but chiefly, and yet not exclusively, we want the thoroughness and the conscientious study of the English schools, where every lesson is a duty to God as well as to man; where not only soundness, but soberness of mind, is inculcated; and where the great end of education is to rear up men to act on better motives than that of rising in the world. American education, as it aims to educate all classes and races, should be, to a certain extent, eclectic. It should combine the best methods of all countries, and adapt them to the exigencies of our free people in order to develop here the ideal American citizen, — the man who prizes character more than reputation, who fears God and loves man.

From this point of observation then, avoiding the rubbish and fossil theories of the past, let us take our start, in order to find more explicitly what a true American education ought to be. As members of the One Holy Catholic and Apostolic Church, we have not far to look. Instinctively we repudiate all theoretical principles, however exalted and apparently scriptural. Trained up, as we have been, to recognize the Trinity that there is in every man, of body, mind, and soul, we cannot call that *education* which only strengthens the muscles, or developes the mental faculties and starves the soul.

Our Prayer-book—our great educator—is the soul's book. It has not one *intellectual* Collect, nor one glorification of man, from the General Confession to the Benediction. Our baptismal theology, too, which has made the Protestant Episcopal Church famed, even among its foes, for its love and care of children, teaches that "the child is father of the man;" and that if our sons and daughters are not to depart from the old way, then they are to be trained up in the way they should go, beginning at the font, and using, at school and college, all the means of grace provided in the Church, to educate, or lead out to their fullest health, all the faculties. A well-trained Churchman cannot run wild after the popular "muscular Christianity" of the passing hour, and seek to bring his child's body to the perfection of a Roman athlete; nor can he stimulate the intellectual faculties exclusively, till our youth, as in some of our best patronized colleges, love to rush in where angels fear to tread, speculating, like Milton's demons in Pandemonium, —

—— "in endless mazes lost."

Neither do we Churchmen endeavor, by a pietistic or a sentimental culture, to develop only the spiritual part of a man. But, by a harmonious and equal education of body, mind, and soul, we seek to "fit a man to perform justly, skilfully, and magnanimously all the offices, both public and private, of peace and war." Education, as we regard it, is the highest and the healthiest development of all the powers of an immortal being. It is not merely the heathenish idea of "*mens sana in corpore sano*," it is the Christian idea of immortality superinduced upon it, and elevating it with all the aspirations and sympathies of a deathless spirit.

The question with us as a Church is not how our children may become prosperous and respectable during their abode on earth, but how they may be made "fellow-citizens of the saints," and fitted for the society of heaven. We do not give way before the present national ambition for intellectual culture exclusively, which, by pounding and polishing a youth's mental calibre for three or four years, expects to develop true greatness of soul, — loyal, reverent, brave, true. So good Bishop Otey preached before the General Convention at Richmond, in 1859, lifting a warning voice against the false principles of education in the United States, by which, as much as by anything, the fearful national punishment of the past four years was incurred. He says (p. 6), "The voice of history proclaims the grave and impressive lesson that the glories of republics have been evanescent, that their energies have become effete and languid in the transmission through fewer generations than those of some hereditary dynasties. They seem to resemble those vegetable productions which bloom more magnificently and bear a richer fruitage, but arrive at earlier decay and decrepitude. How, then, shall we, on whom the care of ours is now incumbent, maintain the vital principle with undiminished healthfulness and vigor, that it may flourish for us, and for those who follow after us? There is but one method, and that is by that plastic touch of an *education* whose moral impress the drippings of time can never efface, nor any stroke of accident destroy. The characters of men do not result from their own investigations; the patterns are not selected and approved by mature judgment: they are formed by the combined development of those associations and sympathies of childhood from whose influence no reasonings or efforts of mature years will ever entirely emancipate them. We must, therefore, infuse into the wave of human society which is to follow us, those principles which will make it pure, and whose absence will cause it to spread bitterness, corruption, and desolation wherever it rolls." The wise Bishop, then, boldly attacks and demolishes the favorite maxim of every social reformer and political aspirant of the day, who reiterate the specious sophism that "Knowledge alone is the unfailing protector of all rights, the nursing parent of all virtues, and the cure of every social malady."

"Show me," he argues (p. 9.), "the *sequence* which is claimed to exist between intellectual wealth and moral purity. Take a child, and teach him the truths of mathematical science. Will you thus make him abhor fraud and falsehood? Teach him natural philosophy, and will you thereby extinguish selfishness and malice, or infuse purity of thought and modesty of demeanor? Teach him the abstractions of moral science, and will you thereby impart the will and power to perform moral duties? Surely not. But now try a different process. Let him be removed from the contact of every irreligious impulse and association. Let him be environed as much as possible by 'whatsoever things are pure, just, true, honest, lovely, and of good report.'" (*Quere:* Could such an environment be found in any of our crowded colleges, where "cram". is the word, not only numerically but intellectually?) "But carry a young man to the Word of God," concludes the Bishop, "for a standard of morals perfect, unalterable, and eternal! Send him to the Throne of Grace, and thither let the teacher repair *with* him and *for* him, and what result may you then rationally anticipate? Instead of the antagonist principle of intelligence and vice mingling harmoniously to make the compound more offensive, you infuse the religious principle, and every thing gross is neutralized and precipitated, every thing noxious is expelled, and the character acquires a permanent purity and transparency."

Such, then, we hold to be true education, in which the soul is never forgotten for an instant, of which the pure and hallowing religion of Jesus is the end and aim, subjecting always the scholar to the Christian, science to revelation, man to God. Religion thus becomes only another word for education, in which God is the teacher: "for religion," as a learned doctor has thoughtfully said (Wiseman's Lectures), "is the great focal point around which the moral world revolves, the all-embracing medium in which every thing moves, increases and lessens; the last refuge of thought, the binding link between the visible and invisible, the revealed and discoverable, the resolution of all anomalies, the determination of all problems in outward nature and in the inward soul, the fixing and steadying element in every science, the blank and object of every meditation."

When the question, therefore, arises before the mind of a Churchman, "How can I best educate my children?" most assuredly he is not to go to the methods and principles of intellectual education alone, which the denominations are always remodelling. He is to seek for school or college where the religious and the churchly element is neither excluded nor tampered with. He is to be anxious for the education of a child's *soul* as well as mind. It is thus the Great Master educates, who said, "Suffer the little children to come unto me;" and again: "Whosoever shall offend one of these little ones that believe in me, it were better that a millstone were hanged about his neck, and he were drowned in the depth of the sea."

And now that we have attempted an answer to some of the questions asked at the outset of this article, we wish to show what has been done, and what is now doing, by the various bodies of Christians around us, and also by our own Church, in this great work of Christian education.

There are 122 endowed colleges in successful operation to-day in our country. Eight of these, in New England, had 2,264 students in 1860–61. If we allow but an average of one hundred undergraduates to each of the colleges outside of New England, we have the approximate result, at least, of ten thousand young men trained every day by non-episcopal adepts and scholars to all the best skill in the various departments of learning. The Congregationalists, who have had the best opportunity ever offered for the almost exclusive education of New England, which has been called "the school-house of America," are this year putting forth redoubled energies. They have resolved to raise $700,000 this year for educational purposes alone, notwithstanding the perfect shower of gold which fell last year, in the shape of legacies, donations, State grants, &c., on Amherst and Yale. Within the past four years, Bowdoin College, Maine, has received $72,000, of which $50,000 was in one donation; Dartmouth College, N. H., has received $47,000; Middlebury College, Vt., has received $10,000; Williams College has received $25,000, — besides it is now erecting some of the noblest buildings in the country for library, chapel, &c.; Amherst College has received more than $100,000, in sums of $60,000, $30,000, and $20,000 each; Harvard, already plethoric with its entailed thousands, received another bequest of $44,000; Andover Theological Seminary has received $50,000, of which $30,000 was from one firm; Yale College has received — including $135,000 from the United-States Government for its Agricultural School — the magnificent sum of $450,000! to which $100,000 was to be added — (the Report states that, of the portion already paid, the following sums have been given by individuals in single donations, viz., $85,000, $50,000, $30,000, $27,000, $25,000, $20,000, $12,000); New-York University has received $60,000; Hamilton College over $100,000; Princeton College, N. J., $130,000, of which $30,000 is in a single donation; Rutgers College, N. J., has received $100,000; Washington University, St. Louis, $50,000, in two donations of $25,000 each, one from New York, the other from Boston; Chicago Theological Seminary has received $80,000; the Protestant College in Syria, $103,000, from American Christians. So that no less than $1,600,000 — and the real truth would put it nearer $2,000,000 — have been cheerfully and spontaneously given to colleges during these years of war. So says the "Independent" of Dec. 1, 1864. According to the Forty-ninth Annual Report of the American Education Society, page 7, "the receipts from donations, legacies, etc., for the year ending April 30, 1865, was $23,386.24. The permanent funds of the Society amount to $81,000.08. The contingent Beneficiary Fund amounts to $25,000."

"We cannot doubt," the Report adds, "that work on a more comprehensive scale awaits us, and that speedily. Many agencies are busy to increase the number of candidates for the Ministry. In 1856, these candidates amounted to 309; in 1860, to 372; in 1865, to 200. Of course, the work done by this American Education Society, under Congregational auspices, is but a very small part of the work done for the training-up of an Evangelical Ministry." We quote from the Forty-ninth Annual Report, page 13. "Never," continues the same Report, on page 14, "has there been a time in the history of this country, when such a wide and effectual door was opened for every form of educational labor."

In the Presbyterian body, the total amount of legacies for the last thirty-three years has been $112,226.39! (pp. 46 and 48, Report of Board of Education). It has aided during that period 3317 candidates for the Ministry. In addition to the receipts from legacies above mentioned, this Society has received, for purposes of general education, since its organization, $106,381.09. For the year ending May 5, 1865, its receipts were $51,308.69. In the State of California, this Society claims (on p. 20, American Report for 1864) to be educating a larger number of classical scholars than any other institution, "Protestant or Catholic." On the first page of its last Report, it is "*Resolved*, that the Assembly earnestly recommend to our congregations the establishment of parochial schools."

In the Methodist denomination, educational efforts have been put forth with all their accustomed zeal. They have 23 colleges, 2 biblical institutes, and 75 seminaries, with over 7,000 students; and they are not left for protection to private or hap-hazard support, as Protestant Episcopal schools and colleges are, but are under the almost exclusive government as well as patronage of the Methodist body. For the correctness of our statistics, we refer to the "Methodist Almanac" for 1865. The truly gigantic book concern is now doing an annual business of over $1,200,000, while its Missionary and Tract and Church-extension Societies and Sunday-school Union have an aggregate income of $1,250,000! The receipts of the Tract Society alone for the year 1863 amounted to $8,718.25. And, as if those almost fabulous figures could not tell the whole truth, add to them the amount of printing, during the year, of Sunday-school books and periodicals, which was equivalent to 469,750,000 pages 18mo, or over two million volumes of two hundred pages each. (See p. 25, "Methodist Almanac" for 1865.)

Add to this the immense circulation of the great newspaper of the Methodists, — one family in every five taking it, while in our Church only one family in thirty takes a Church paper, — and we are ready to acquiesce in the statement of the preacher, at the recent Centenary Celebration of American Methodism; viz., "The Methodists have supplied the land with greater educational facilities than any other Christian denomination in the same space of time." Within the past few weeks, preliminary steps have been taken to establish a Scientific School in connection with the Wesleyan College at Middletown. Two millions is the thank-offering confidently expected for the Centenary of American Methodism.

The Baptists have been only less prolific in the work of education. They have 23 colleges in successful operation, and 11 theological institutions. The total receipts of the American Baptist Publication Society for 1865 were $153,954.93. Twenty-eight new publications have been issued during the year, making the total issues of the year as follows: Books, tracts, etc., 1,399,500 copies, making 48,126,150 18mo pages. In Providence, twenty men gave $10,000 each, total $200,-000, for the farther endowment of the already wealthy Brown University; and, as if this were not enough, another endowment is counted as secure, as the following extract from the "New-York Examiner" will show: —

"We learn from a brief notice in the 'Watchman and Reflector,' that, at a late meeting of the Social Union, a Boston Baptist gathering, a principle subject of discussion was the endowment of Brown University; and that Dr. Sears, who was present, called for $300,000 as the addition of the funds now required. Of the importance of this endowment we could not speak in terms which would overstate our convictions; and we trust that the wealth of New-England Baptists will hasten the perfect consummation of this measure. We do not, however, direct attention in this instance so much to the importance of the endowment, as to the significance of these growing figures. When this measure began to be agitated, we think it was but half this sum which it was proposed to raise. Before the work can be accomplished, the sum is doubled. This doubling is perfectly in harmony with the unprecedented growth of wealth and of prices, and is an imperative necessity. Woe be to us if our colleges are not kept in relation with the progress of our times! A succession of competent teachers cannot be maintained in Providence, and the enlargement of facilities be made equal to the demands of society, without the addition of all this, and more. Educated talent is in requisition for purposes which pay largely; and, if teachers are but half paid, the class will sink to the level of the pay, and so the very sources of intellectual life be dried up."

As to the schools and colleges of the Roman Catholics, every one knows that they are the mainstay and stronghold of Romanism in this country. In almost every valley, in every large city or town, the Parish School or the Female Seminary is built close by the church. One million dollars has been received from the Roman Catholics of Europe within the past few years, as we are credibly informed, for schools in the West alone. Now if this be not the wisdom of the serpent, then we cannot imagine what is. Their statistics are kept jesuitically concealed from unsuspicious Protestants; and, with a patience and foresight worthy of a better cause, they labor to insure the ultimate triumph of Romanism on this continent by beginning with the boys, and especially with the girls. A gentleman from the Indian Territory thus writes the Secretary of the Domestic Board: —

"Permit me to make another suggestion. My apology is, that I have had ten years' experience in the West, seven of them in the *far West.*

"The Church of Rome has had her Female Schools in every promising and available place throughout this great region. She is now reaping a bountiful harvest from the seed thus sown. We have done next to nothing in this way. We have spent tens of thousands upon Gambier, Griswold, and Racine, but nothing upon a large — may I say *remunerating* — scale for girls. We have been impolitic, and are losing *young men* every day, by not having provided Church girls with a marketable standard of education.

"My dear doctor, you and the Committee will, perhaps, laugh at the expression; but let me say that it is strictly true. I could fill ten pages in confirmation of this fact, if you had time to read them. Give us female Church schools, with earnest teachers and low-priced tuition, and we will take deep root in all these far Western States.

"Bishops Talbot and Vail are opening their eyes to this fact. Thank God that they are! And Bishop Coxe is proposing two such schools for his diocese. My heart leaped with joy at the announcement.

"If we can plant one good Female Seminary in every Western State, we shall soon have the families of our leading citizens friendly to, if not members of, our Church. Without this auxiliary, we must plod on for decades."

The Roman Catholic Church in the United States is divided into seven Provinces, and each Province is subdivided into five or six Dioceses, upon an average. These Dioceses have generally their own colleges, seminaries, and various institutions of learning, in successful operation. We give a few extracts from one or two of these Diocesan Reports, taken from "Sadlier's Catholic Almanac & Ordo" for the year 1866.

Beginning with the Diocese of Baltimore, to which "prerogative of place" is granted by Pio Nono, we observe that five pages of the Almanac, 12mo, are crowded with its College and School Statistics. The Theological Seminary and St. Mary's University, Baltimore, has 65 students; St. Charles's College, near Ellicott's Mills, has 115 students: Georgetown College; Zinzaga College, D. C.; Loyola College, Baltimore; Mount St. Mary's College, near Emmitsburg; and Borromeo College, Pikesville, — are well sustained. In addition, there are 11 convents, 5 female literary institutions, and 37 pay and free schools. The Academy of St. Joseph has 300 pupils; St. Michael's Parish School, 1,100; the Benevolent Schools for girls at the Visitation Convents in Georgetown and Frederick, 195 pupils.

In the Diocese of New York, four pages of schools and colleges are given. St. Joseph's Theological Seminary has 98 students; De la Salle Institute has 324 pupils; Convents of the Sacred Heart, 364 scholars; St. Mary's School, East Broadway, pupils 180; St. Peter's School, Barclay Street, pupils 100; Academy of the Holy Cross, Forty-second Street, pupils 223.

In the Diocese of Cincinnati, besides the usual amount of colleges, we find 13 pay and free schools, with scholars counted by thousands, viz.: St. Xavier's School for boys, pupils 528; St. Paul's School for boys, pupils 830; St. Francis's School for boys and girls, pupils 1,000; St. John's School for boys and girls, pupils 900; St. Mary's School for boys and girls, pupils 877.

The Diocese of New Orleans has its 3 colleges, 10 academies for boys, and 20 academies for young ladies, and parochial schools. The Diocese of Albany is fairly crowded with schools. The Cathedral School has 270 girls; St. John's, Schenectady, has 540 pupils; St. Peter's, Troy, has 500 pupils; St. Bernard's, Cohoes, has 600 pupils. Add to these 31 academies and schools, counting their pupils by hundreds.

The Diocese of Cleveland has its 7 academies and 70 schools.

The Diocese of Buffalo has 4 ecclesiastical institutions; 26 religious institutions; 22 literary institutions, 5 for boys and 17 for girls.

The Diocese of Chicago has one university, 9 academies for young ladies.

The Diocese of Milwaukee has one ecclesiastical seminary, 2 male academies, 6 female academies. The Diocese of St. Louis has 2 ecclesiastical seminaries, 7 academies, with hundreds of pupils, 4 colleges, at one of which, "the College of the Christian Brothers," there are 600 students.

The Diocese of Philadelphia reports 3 colleges, and 23 academies and select schools. The Brothers of the 23 Christian schools report 2,000 scholars. Of course, these figures give but a bare outline of the work done by Rome in schools and colleges. We can only refer to the "Almanac & Ordo" for 1866, in which 181 pages, 12mo, are filled with merely the names of priests, teachers, and schools.

And now compare the work of our own beloved Church with these energetic bodies. Compare our five or six colleges with even the twenty-three colleges of Methodism. We struck down roots in America but five or six years after the Methodists got foothold. Why, then, this marked superiority in zeal and liberality and success? At least, we ought to be "provoked to good works" by the dozens of great colleges, such as Yale, Harvard, Amherst, Williams, and Dartmouth, which claim affinity with Congregationalism. The fact that they have secured such advantage by long possession of the land — which is more than nine points in college law — ought to stir us to greater exertion in undertaking new educational enterprises, as well as to heap up the endowments of our established institutions. Where would American Unitarianism be to-day, if its main-stay, which is Harvard College, were to part from her theological moorings, as she has done before? And where will the Protestant Episcopal Church stand hereafter among the surrounding denominations, unless we can have our own schools and colleges? No man can need argument to convince him, that the Church which cannot educate her own children does not deserve, and cannot win, success. But compare our statistics, which follow, with those which precede. It may be that figures will speak louder than words, in calling our prosperous Laymen and apathetic Presbyters to come to the help of the Lord against the negative Christianity and unhealthy education which obtains in so many schools and colleges of our country.

Our statistics are not easy to get at by any Layman. Even a Bishop would be obliged, as we are, to send for Reports and Catalogues in all directions; while the more politic denominations keep their statistical information before the people, by publishing them in their Almanacs, carefully summed up. In fact, it has been so difficult to find out the actual work of our Church in this matter of education, that we sincerely hope the following attempt may draw forth, by way of criticism or addition, something now inaccessible.

We begin with Trinity College, at Hartford, Conn. It was founded in 1824. It has, perhaps, the finest location for a college in the country, situated in the heart of New England, on the beautiful city park. It has an available capital of nearly $200,000, in addition to real estate valued at $300,000. Within the past two years, $100,000 has been added to its endowment; thus placing it, as Bishop Williams said in his Report to Convention, " on a new basis, and opens to it, I fondly hope, a future of greatly enlarged prosperity. Under its accomplished head, and with its departments well provided for, it can challenge, as well as ask, the confidence and support of Churchmen. These granted, there is no limit that can be set to its influence and usefulness." Its graduates number about six hundred. Nearly half of these, or one-tenth of all our Clergy in the United States, have been, or have become, candidates for the Ministry at "Trinity;" a fact which speaks volumes for the healthiness of the discipline, and which surely ought to give "Trinity" a claim on all loyal as well as prudent Churchmen. The present number of undergraduates is sixty.

Hobart College, since its foundation in 1826, has actually done half as much for the Ministry of the Church as Yale, and one-third as much as Columbia has in five times the number of years (vol. iv. Ch. Rev. p. 248). Let earnest Churchmen know and ponder such a fact, and let them not despise the comparatively small numbers at "Trinity" and "Hobart;" for they are quite on an average with other colleges in the first years of their existence, as the following table will show, and that notwithstanding the large number of Episcopal students now at other institutions. The first of the following columns shows the number graduated during the first twenty years, and the second column shows the number that entered the Ministry:—

	Graduates.	Ministers.
Harvard	130	66
Yale	108	70
Princeton	291	137
Columbia	110	20
Williams	434	146
Dartmouth	262	112
Brown's	101	36
Union	415	109
Trinity	296	120
Hobart	91	29

p. 219, vol. iv. *Church Review.*

If the twenty-five Episcopalians that have been graduated yearly at Harvard and Yale, to say nothing of other New-England colleges, had been students at our only Church college in New-England, its Alumni would have numbered eight hundred instead of three hundred. And the same principle holds true in reference to Hobart. And the question therefore is, How much stronger would our Church have been to-day than it is, if Churchmen had patronized their own institutions, as other denominations of Christians have done?

Hobart College reports eighty-four undergraduates, with an able faculty, and with the standard of scholarship and discipline fully equal to the capacities of any young man to endure: it certainly ought to count its students by hundreds. From De Veaux College, Suspension Bridge, we have received no report, although we are informed that its affairs are in prosperous condition.

Columbia College, "the president of which must be a member of, and in communion with, the Protestant

Episcopal Church," does not, however, exclusively belong to our Chuch; and does not give the prominence to the religious element in education, for which our other Church colleges wish to be distinguished. The number of students in 1860–61 was two hundred and one. In the far West, "Griswold College" is getting strong foundations. "Nashotah" has thirty-three students and ninety-three alumni: it is one of the few educational glories of our Church; and would not live a great while unendowed, and "on nothing for the morrow," if Churchmen knew their responsibilities. Faribault has a bright future.

Kenyon College, Gambier, Ohio, has sixty-eight students. In the theological department there are fifteen students. One academy and one seminary complete the list for Ohio, given in the "Church Almanac." The Assistant Bishop has just succeeded in adding over $100,000 to the endowment, as we are very happy to learn; and a chapel has been recently pledged to him by his old parishioners of Ascension Church, which will enable the trustees to convert the present chapel into Rosse Hall, for library, cabinet, and a general hall for college uses.

Racine College proper was established, by the union with it of St. John's Hall, Nashotah, in 1859; and, in the six years of its existence, has done a noble work. In healthy, thorough, churchly culture, it ranks among the very first. It has no endowment, and yet its income the past year has been $41,000. The number of students is one hundred and thirty-eight. Surely its great success ought to convince the trustees of "Trinity,"

"Hobart," &c., if they need it, that sound and thorough and fearless Church principles, not held in abeyance, but made prominent, are better props for a college than even endowments. The object of Racine College "is to educate the youth placed in it through the agency of the Church of the living God, and in the principles of the Catholic faith as held by the Protestant Episcopal Church in the United States." The plan at "Racine," as stated in a letter to a friend, written by the Principal, is to train up the youth committed to its care: 1st, Physically, with proper attention to all manly games and sports; 2d, To mould and govern and sustain the whole system by the influence of the order and life of the Holy Catholic Church. "Racine" deserves honor for at least "showing its colors," and living or dying with its principles made prominent.

Norwich University, Vermont, proposes to live on its distinguishing features, which are—"Military Science and Tactics, together with full Scientific and Classical curricula." Its undergraduates number sixty-seven. Its success, under the able management of Dr. Bourns, leads many to regret that he proposes to resign in favor of some less experienced, but more warlike, military general. The University has no endowment. The Vermont Episcopalian Institute is another witness to the fact, that sound principles succeed where endowments fail. It has been in operation only five years. Only the Willoughby Professorship is endowed to the amount of $10,000. Since its opening, it has sent forth ninety-three pupils. Its present number is forty-three, its full limit. Thirty-one applications beyond its ability to receive have been made since last November. Its beautiful grounds and buildings are valued at $25,000.

St. Paul's School, Concord, the model-school for New-England Churchmen, overflows, with its discipline and scholarship for principal attractions. "The religious education of the boys, though regarded as of the highest consequence, has not been made a matter of routine. It is pursued in quietness and simplicity, never offending the consciences of those who do not belong to the Church, yet never departing from the paths of pleasantness and peace, to which the Church directs her children." The land and buildings consist of an estate of seventy-seven acres; a large and commodious house, with numerous outbuildings; an appropriate chapel; a library and cabinet. The total endowment is about $75,000. It commenced April 30, 1856, with three boys, and completes the first decade of its existence with about two hundred names on its list, — fifty-five in attendance, — and eight teachers.

St. Stephen's College, Annandale, was founded for the special work of preparing men for the General Theological Seminary, in 1862. It has now thirty-eight students, and has been obliged to deny admission to twenty, for want of room. The property belonging to the College, in land and buildings, amounts to about $70,000. A building is just about to be commenced, as a residence for the Warden, which is to cost $70,000. An effort is also being made to raise $100,000. An income of $5000 is pledged to be continued until this endowment is completed.

The Berkley School, in Connecticut, is a great success, under the efficient control of the Bishop. The whole number of its alumni is ninety-six. Its undergraduates now number twenty. Of these, six are graduates of Trinity, one from Yale, and three from other colleges. These last figures are a fair illustration of the benefit of preferring other colleges to our own, especially if we consider that there are always about as many sons of Churchmen at "Yale" as at "Trinity."

Old Cheshire Academy, "delightfully situated," as we use to term it in college days, is in the highest degree of prosperity for a Church school. And, by prosperity for a Church school, we mean that its existence, and superior attractions as a Church institution, are known and appreciated. Over one hundred pupils are actually in attendance. New buildings have recently been erected, and a promising effort is actually on foot for its endowment.

The Rectory School, at Hamden, Conn., is another of the prominent and very successful schools of "the land of steady habits": it is always full, and ranks very high in thoroughness of discipline and scholarship. The Deer-Hill Institute, Danbury, and St. Paul's School, Brookfield, deserve more honorable mention than we have space to give them. In the matter of Church schools, old Connecticut is, in political phrase, "the Banner State." Among the general societies for educational purposes, the Society for the Increase of the Ministry presents a very attractive record. Every Churchman in the land should read its last Annual

Report. Its name indicates its object. It has assisted, since 1859, two hundred and eight scholars. During the past year, it has rendered aid to one hundred and six students, from twenty-one Dioceses. Its receipts last year were $15,027. The General Theological Seminary, with its immensely valuable property, is just emerging from the embarrassments of the past few years. It is the pride of our Church; and, with its nine hundred and sixteen alumni, its possibilities for good, and its great wealth in real estate, who can estimate the power of such an institution in the past, present, or future? Its present number of students is fifty-nine; volumes in the library, 13,640. The farthest half of the Seminary Quadrangle, which was formerly a receptacle for ashes, has recently been sold for $90,000. $10,000 income has been secured, since the last meeting of the Board of Trustees, by sales, leases, and presents. Bishop Coxe has also succeeded in raising $23,000 for a new Professorship.

The Lord be praised for all the zeal and self-sacrifice, and noble liberality, of which these foregoing statistics are proof! They are an earnest of what our Church will yet accomplish after we have more fully realized our responsibilities and privileges. We love to flatter ourselves that the present essay will help to such a realization, in which we have tried to gather, and lay before the eye of the Church, the work accomplished by other Christian bodies, as a contrast with our endeavors, and as a provocative "to love and good works." Our growing and generous Church, as we love to think, only needs to be told what has been done, and what remains to do.

The difficulty in getting at even these few statistics must be our apology, if any complain of omission or partial statement.

Enough have been secured, we think, to show that the Protestant Episcopal Church is very far behind the measure of her ability in this matter. Surely no one can be so short-sighted as to conclude that we, as a Church, are so distanced in the race, that we must give up the education of our youth to the Sectarian or Infidel or Papal teachers of our country. Even if we have no superior principles of education for which to strive, still we are bound to do our share as *a* Church, if not as *the* Church. Where would the Church of England be to-day, if Oxford had been Unitarian, or Cambridge had been Papal? or if, as in the larger proportion of American colleges, religious culture were excluded from the college course, — unless the mockery of chapel service, with its tobacco juice and rolling pennies, is religious culture? What is college life, or school life, or any kind of life, without the Bible and Prayer-book, or some devotional book for regular study and meditation? How can a young man be said to be educated, if for four years his soul sleeps, or is slowly poisoned to death? Says "Tom Brown at Oxford" (p. 105, vol. i.), "Oxford and Cambridge, and our great schools, are the heart of dear old England." "Did you ever read," he asks, "Secretary Cook's address to the Vice-Chancellor, Doctors, &c.? No? Well, listen then. And he went to his bookcase, took down a book, and read: 'The very truth is, that all wise princes respect the welfare of their estates, and consider that schools and universities are, as in the body, the noble and vital part, which, being vigorous and sound, send good blood and active spirit into the veins and arteries, which cause health and strength; or, if feeble and ill-affected, corrupt the vital parts, whereupon grow diseases, and, in the end, death itself. *A low standard up here for ten years may corrupt half the parishes in the kingdom.*' "

What, then, has become of the common prudence and foresight of the Protestant Episcopal Church, which spends hundreds of thousands of dollars every year on the education of her children at non-episcopal institutions, thereby supporting a mighty influence, which is exerted against the Church, and made to obstruct her growth through all the ramifications of society? "And Joab took Amasa by the beard with the right hand, and kissed him. But Amasa took no heed to the sword that was in Joab's hand; so he smote him therewith under the fifth rib, and struck him not again, and he died" (2 Sam. xx. 10). In order to give *my* son what are called superior advantages at a college without healthy religious life, I do all in my power to destroy *his* son, and *his* son's son, by forgetting even the instinct of self-preservation, and by accepting the American sophisms, that "numbers are the test of worth;" and that "intellectual culture alone is healthy education," no matter whether Jesuit or Unitarian or Atheist teach.

"Numbers," says Dr. Hitchcock, president of Amherst, "only show the estimation in which a college is held by the public, but do not settle its real worth"

(p. 43, Life, &c.) ; and he adds : "Sometimes the reason why a college overflows with students is, that it has lowered the standard of scholarship or of discipline more than other institutions." Besides, great numbers prevent the only kind of discipline which is healthy, and which is described in "Tom Brown at Oxford," when he asked Hardy the secret of the improvement at St. Ambrose. "I've no secret," says Hardy, "except taking a real interest in all that the men do, and living with them as much as I can." Now, excessive numbers prevent all such personal contact and sympathy; and hence our Church colleges, "Trinity," "Hobart," *et al.*, claim a healthier discipline, and a higher, because healthier, tone of scholarship, for the two are inseparable. Cramming a diseased soul is like fatting a *Pate de fois gras.* It is a diseased liver. Lose not your sons, therefore, in a crowd, by perilling their soul's interest during the four most trying years of their lives. Revivals of religion, as they are called, like tornadoes, are periodically arranged to excite, and sweep them away from the "path of peace" into the world. Temptations, which a Moses or a Peter could hardly have resisted, encompass them just at the time when all home restraints are gone, and when the old Prayer-book and Bible are heard only on "the sabbath" or at hurried chapel.

Is it then marvellous, that, while thousands of the laity who are not thus educated are flocking into the old Church from all denominations of Christians, yet five hundred parishes to-day want Clergymen, who are not to be found, because educated by the American method of soul starvation and mental stimulus? If Churchmen do not patronize their own institutions, who will? If, on the contrary, they equip them with fair endowments, and send their children to fill them, why, of course, they will soon outrank the best in the land, and prove a most efficient means of propagating far and wide that moderate and conservative tone of thought and action on which the future of our country and Church depends.

But are not the Clergy, after all, responsible for the success of our principles of education in America? For can they not, in most cases, secure any child in the Parish for any school in which the Rector takes a lively interest? He can disabuse the parent's mind of the false opinion, that numbers are preferable to principles, and intellect to be desired rather than character. The schools and colleges of our Church belong to our Clergy. If they are not respectable in numbers or wealth or culture, then help make them so, as the earnest Baptist, Congregational, Methodist, and Papist Pastors work for their own institutions. Establish Professorships, and fill them with the best talent in the land. Enrich their libraries; found scholarships. A little impulse to public sentiment would at once endow "Trinity," "Hobart," and "Kenyon" with a half-million each, and win the hundred per cent. return to the Church. Already these colleges and schools of which we have spoken have done more to build up the Dioceses in which they are located than any other influences. Bishop Berkley and Elihu Yale saw this when they founded Yale College; and if the Bishop's principles of education had been acted on at Yale since its foundation, then would not the Protestant Episcopal Church have been to-day, in reality, "The American Catholic Church"? But let our comparative remissness in the mighty work of Christian education lead us to redeem the time we have lost.

All that is now needed is a thorough appreciation of the greatness of the work of true education; and as a help to such appreciation, we offer these principles and facts for the thoughtful consideration of intelligent Churchmen.

www.ingramcontent.com/pod-product-compliance
Lightning Source LLC
LaVergne TN
LVHW011125110826
845150LV00008B/2256
* 9 7 8 1 4 1 8 1 9 5 0 5 2 *